Positive Thinking To Transform Yourself

The Art of Marginal Gains

Table of content

Introduction

First of all, a big thank you for downloading this tutorial. This indicates that you are eager to learn more about the strength and a system for taking constructive action in your life. This is without a doubt one of the most powerful and successful methods you can use to empower, support, and develop your company, way of life, and personality for years to come.However, in order to be optimistic, you must have the proper mindset. We will look at this mindset in more detail in this book and make sure we can impart it to people around us. Positivity must be the driving force behind all we do and everything we hope to accomplish.

We'll explain why that optimism is important and how you can apply it in this section. More significantly, we will outline the five key areas of your life that a positive outlook may enhance. We'll show you how to alter your lifestyle, thinking, emotions, level of fitness, and level of productivity. You may infuse your whole existence with a more optimistic outlook on the world by using these suggestions and techniques.You will find a lot of support and advantages in this book, making it simpler than ever to alter your perspective and attitude. You'll get assistance withIdeas for maintaining your fitness and getting started on the path to a healthier, more equitable condition of body and mindMental practices that help you go ahead with the greatest mentality possible in order to change and better your life emotional support, ensuring that you can comprehend how to maintain mental clarity when it is most necessary.

Plans and routines for your lifestyle that are aimed at making you more consistent and stable in your life and the world around youPersonal practices that will undoubtedly alter the way you act, think, and liveBy utilizing this book, you may be certain that your life and career will continue to develop in a constant and ongoing manner.To help you get through difficult days and make sure you can always be at your best, improve your body, mind, and mindset.

Look more physically fit, healthier, and content overall. Give your body and mind the support they need to perform at their best.

Fitness Objectives and Routines

It's important to start with the focal point, which is your body, before moving on. We're going to examine how you can improve your life in terms of productivity and achieving your objectives. I discovered, though, that my body was not capable of facilitating change, so my mind was not prepared for it.

I therefore researched the fitness objectives and routines I wanted to try and imitate. When I started this program, I quickly realized that the advice below had helped me reshape, strengthen, and improve my body.

Taking daily walks

Why will this cause me to change for the better?

The first thing I suggest you look into is taking daily walks. A great way to give the body extra exercise is to walk every day.

Applying the Technique for More Positive Thinking

When you first wake up and are ready to go, just go for a walk. A quick stroll can help increase blood flow and clarity.

How Often Should I Workout?

each day! There is no way I would ever advise getting rid of this. It's an incredibly helpful approach to refining your physique and making sure it's in top functional shape.

Without this change, life would be very different.

More days will begin for you with a lack of enthusiasm and confidence. Days without activity have a tendency to be drowsy, languid, and often tense.

Living Through This Change

However, by merely going for a morning stroll, you guarantee that you receive some exercise. Exercise produces endorphins, which improve our mood and mental acuity. Walking every day can really improve your mood!

Active Living: How Will This Change My Attitude?

I discovered that using a computer forced me to spend the majority of my time sitting at home. I got better by getting up and exercising for 5 minutes every 30 minutes.

Applying the Technique for More Positive Thinking

To prevent any circulation issues, I would just get up and take a little stroll about the workplace, generally up and down some stairs.

How Often Should I Workout?

every 30 minutes. However, even if you just perform it once every hour, you'll see a little increase in the level of your general fitness over time.

Without this change, life would be very different.

My legs would often start most of my days with a lot of pain running through them and little motion. As I grow older, this will only become worse.

Living Through This Change

My life has altered as a result of this. Now that I am much more mobile and my days are busier than ever before, even my early morning walks feel better than they ever have!

Will clarifying my why make me happier?

I discovered that I could work the majority of my body in only 10 minutes and give myself a much-needed workout. Exercises for strength alone were quite helpful.

Applying the Technique for More Positive Thinking

I discovered that working out different parts of my body each day—my chest, legs, arms, thighs, etc.—really helped to lift my spirits. Additionally, I felt more confident and fit!

How Often Should I Workout?

I would advise you to do the same, as I do it daily. Your mind will function much more quickly, and your body will feel stronger as a result.

Without this change, life would be very different.

I just discovered that my level of fitness was gradually declining. Without doing this, my body would continue to feel weak and sluggish, and my strength would continue to decline.

Living Through This Change

Every morning, I feel considerably more aware and sharp than I did.

I feel better capable of handling bodily issues without having to exert so much effort.

Why Will This Help Me Become More Positive? Jogging on the Spot

Simply jogging on the spot throughout a TV show was a terrific little solution I discovered. I like to exercise while watching soccer.

Applying the Technique for More Positive Thinking

I just need to get up and begin running. I find that since I am focusing on the TV, I am using less mental energy and can thus carry on.

How Often Should I Workout?

I repeat: I do this every day. I feel that it really improves my entire quality of life, and my cardio is already starting to get better.

Without this change, my condition would have only gotten worse; instead, this training regimen encourages me to pay closer attention to my general endurance and makes it simpler for me to maintain a more optimum level of fitness.

Living Through This Change

Prior to this, I spent a significant portion of my time watching TV and staring at screens. This little adjustment has completely changed the way I operate, increasing both my output and cardiovascular fitness.

Bedtime activities

Why will this cause me to change for the better?

If that describes you, then spending a little extra "personal time" with a loved one would be ideal. Just by having more sex, you'll feel more powerful!

Applying the Technique for More Positive Thinking

Regular sex is fantastic for relieving stress and may even be used to heal illnesses since it strengthens the immune system over time.

How Often Should I Workout?

Okay, do what you can! There isn't a set quantity required, but more than what you already do should be a good substitute; it truly depends on you.

Without this change, life would be very different.

Well, you raise your risk of having poorer cardiovascular health, and according to some research, it may even significantly increase your risk of developing prostate cancer.

Living Through This Change

I just have a higher quality of life; I sleep better; and my body is in much less discomfort. We feel more at ease with one another as my connection has grown.

Establishing a Habit: How Will This Make Me More Positive?

Nevertheless, using a habit was one of the most effective strategies I discovered for helping yourself. I started playing puzzle games, and it truly helped make my thinking sharper.

Applying the Technique for More Positive Thinking

I decided to take up a new activity since it truly helps us to improve our lifestyle and health. Trying new things is beneficial for the soul.

How Often Should I Workout?

Depending on what you do, as often as possible.For instance, if you want to join a sports team, be sure to give it your all.

Without this change, life would be very different.

Simply put, your existence will be far less exciting, and you'll likely get more irritated and upset by the few experiments you do have. This brings about some very intriguing variability.

Living Through This Change

But as a result of this adjustment, you'll start to feel much more at ease with yourself. As you begin to overcome and take on new problems in life, it gives your life more diversity and guarantees that you'll continue to experience constant success.

Places to park

Why will this cause me to change for the better?

Now I park a few streets away if I need to go to the workplace or the shops. It increases the walking time by 2 to 3 minutes, which is helpful.

Applying the Technique for More Positive Thinking

Simply because it's wonderful to get a little more exercise, I decided to do this.

It also gives me time to think before I have to go participate.

How Often Should I Workout?

wherever you go outside. I discovered that it was a really easy habit to form that would progressively increase fitness while promoting mental relaxation.

Without this change, life would be very different.

It won't make a world of difference, but it's just one more thing you can do to help; without it, nothing you do will matter.

Living Through This Change

You'll feel more physically fit, have less mental clutter when you go to work or shop, etc., and you'll feel better about yourself and your physique in general.

Stretching as directed

Why will this cause me to change for the better?

I discovered that stretching for 5 minutes after a shower or upon awakening was one of the most effective strategies for me to improve my state of fitness.

Applying the Technique for More Positive Thinking

Simply getting out of bed allowed me to stretch my arms, neck, back, legs, calves, and hamstrings. It just took a little while!

How Often Should I Workout?

each and every morning. It enables you to leave the house without experiencing all of the aches and pains that the majority of us experience throughout the day. very helpful for promoting physical recovery from pain.

Without this change, life would be very different.

It won't be a big deal if you don't do this, but if you want to be in shape, every little bit helps.

Living Through This Change

You'll wake up less tired and aching, and you'll be more likely to accomplish your daily goals without experiencing any negative side effects.

Why will working together make me more positive?

Are you having trouble getting in shape? Then you need to think about joining a friend for a run. Your fitness may be greatly improved with a jogging partner.

Applying the Technique for More Positive Thinking

After a few weeks of practice, I discovered that simply going for that morning run with a buddy was wonderful for spirits and general pleasure.

How Often Should I Workout?

Circumstances may arise whenever you and your partner are able, but they shouldn't ever be a hindrance to your progress. Just be careful to schedule it when you can, together.

Without this change, life would be very different.

You could find it more difficult to stick to your fitness objectives, and you might be more likely than others to give up when things become difficult or when you reach a plateau.

Living Through This Change

You'll likely be in better physical and mental shape. Working with a friend makes it simpler to get through the day and exercise.

Adding fun to exercise

Why will this cause me to change for the better?

Making exercise enjoyable was my biggest fitness difficulty, and I discovered that joining a sports team was the perfect solution. I found that just by playing soccer, I started to like working out.

Applying the Technique for More Positive Thinking Three times a week, I go to practice, and on Sundays, I play. Whatever sport or activity you choose to become involved in, you'll find something that appeals to you.

How Often Should I Workout?

The majority of individuals feel at ease practicing three or four evenings each week. As a result, your whole training and fitness regimen becomes more encouraging since you are motivated to accomplish it.

Without this change, life would be very different.

Life without this will be difficult if you are someone who must exercise or stay in shape for a certain cause. Training becomes more "meaningful" when there is a purpose, such as in sports.

Living Through This Change

You'll feel better physically, be happier emotionally, and be prepared to take on the world. In the long run, your overall quality of life will improve significantly.

Mental Practices

My mentality has always been a significant barrier in my quest to overcome negativity and become more optimistic. I thus made the decision to confront my mind and take a big and significant risk. I considered how I conceptualized ideas and how that could have prevented me from moving forward.

To be honest, the responses I received were very astounding. I discovered that by implementing the modifications listed below, my life would become far more consistent. Each piece of advice will guarantee that you form constructive, proactive mental habits that will give you a winning attitude.

Considering the negative

Why will this cause me to change for the better?

But one of the most effective adjustments you can make is to alter your overall perspective of the world, particularly your attitude toward negativity.

Applying the Technique for More Positive Thinking

I just began to stop and think about how miserable I had been all day. I became aware of how often I would make bad decisions—every day!

How Often Should I Workout?

Everyday. I discovered that being conscious of my mentality was the simplest approach to moderating it. If I realize how unfavorable I am, I may change.

Without this change, life would be very different.

You'll simply keep having bad ideas run through your head. If you wish to prevent this, simply consider creating time for thinking.

Living Through This Change

The major reason I would advise making this adjustment is because it will make you more conscious of your mindset and how much it needs to change.

Why Will This Help Me Become More Positive? Considering Success

Simply being able to imagine what can happen in the future is a strong tool that can enhance your attitude. Thinking about success is a terrific notion.

Applying the Technique for More Positive Thinking

The simplest method to achieve this is to just reflect on your most recent accomplishments for a while—even for five minutes. Even if you haven't achieved "success" yet, keep thinking in this manner.

How Often Should I Workout?

whenever you are discouraged about your position and development. You'll find it much simpler to stay on track with who you are by making a little modification.

Without this change, life would be very different.

You'll just keep ignoring the positive aspects of your life and allowing them to pass you by. Consider how you achieved success.

Living Through This Change

But if you take the time to make this adjustment, you'll be much more proud of your development. Keep in mind that changing anything positive takes time, including your own mindset!

Relational Thoughts

Why will this cause me to change for the better?

But one of the best adjustments I ever made to my life was how often I would stop and think. I used to make poor decisions on instinct.

Applying the Technique for More Positive Thinking

I, along with you, may become more optimistic by switching to reflection before acting. While taking action often entails responding to the drawbacks, it also helps you recognize the positives.

How Often Should I Workout?

each day! I discovered that merely spending a little amount of time each day examining where I was in my head helped me concentrate.

Without this change, life would be very different.

I soon realized that if I didn't do this, my life would typically grow more perplexing, and I would waste too much time just responding to circumstances without information.

Living Through This Change

I was able to cease making errors because of this little modification. I take fewer chances and am more measured now, basing my decisions on reality rather than embellishments.

Remarking on Your Positive

Why will this cause me to change for the better?

How frequently do you genuinely recall being optimistic in your mind? It's one of the most positive things you can do to express your optimism.

Applying the Technique for More Positive Thinking

I just discovered that looking at a joyful memory for five minutes in the morning was a fantastic approach to shifting my perspective from negative to positive.

How Often Should I Workout?

each and every morning. You can get out of bed with a smile rather than a scowl on your face by recalling any event in your life.

Without this change, life would be very different.

It's quite OK if you decide that you don't need this at all in your life. Others will feel far more at ease making this move, however.

Living Through This Change

Simply reflecting on positive prior events for five minutes can help you feel much more at ease with who you are and where you're going.

Identifying the advantages

Why will this cause me to change for the better?

One issue that I and other people often have is always focusing on the disadvantages of a circumstance. But why not start seeking solutions instead of focusing on the issue?

Applying the Technique for More Positive Thinking

Simply change your perspective on any issue. Instead of bemoaning the issue's presence, start looking into workable ideas that might assist you in later fixing it!

How Often Should I Workout?

For a time, I had to do this task almost every day. But eventually, it became automatic, and I stopped complaining about problems and began to value discovering answers.

Without this change, life would be very different.

You'll never stop believing that everything is against you and that there is nothing you can do to improve your situation. Without this modification, negativity will rule.

Living Through This Change

But if you adopt this new perspective, they will be seen for what they are: issues. You'll keep your feet on the ground more often and probably solve problems more quickly.

Doubting Assumptions

Why will this cause me to change for the better?

How frequently do you question your assumptions regarding a particular circumstance? If not, now is the time to start. You'll be able to keep evolving if you challenge your preconceptions.

Applying the Technique for More Positive Thinking

It's quite simple to never question our views and presumptions, yet doing so could be unnecessarily pessimistic. Instead, consider if that line of thinking is valid and why it exists.

How Often Should I Workout?

whenever you see your thoughts spiraling downward in a bad direction. Go online and seek out information on the issue that has you so concerned. Is your first assumption still true today?

Without this change, life would be very different.

Many people avoid taking this path because they don't want to be corrected. But being incorrect is not a bad thing—just another opportunity to learn!

Living Through This Change

You'll experience far less entrenchment and be less prone to feel threatened by disagreement. One of the best things you can do is what you're doing.

Why Will This Help Me Become More Positive? Accepting Your Success

Many people, including myself for a very long time, find it difficult to accept achievement. We want to believe that it was a mistake or that chance played a role.

Applying the Technique for More Positive Thinking

If this is how you feel, ask a few individuals whose opinions you trust to respond honestly the next time the thought crosses your mind.

How Often Should I Workout?

whenever you sense a confidence crisis developing. It's a risky issue that, most likely, will only make you feel worse. Asking whenever it's on will help you avoid it.

Without this change, life would be very different.

While focusing only on your failures, you'll continue to undermine your accomplishments. This fosters negativity and is the opposite of what a positive, action-driven existence requires.

Living Through This Change

You'll become much more at ease with yourself and conscious of your life's victories and setbacks. By doing so, you'll be able to advance without always believing that you're failing.

Examining Your Errors

Why will this cause me to change for the better?

Finding answers will be a lot simpler if you take the time to consider why you failed. Many of us are aware of our failures, but why?

Applying the Technique for More Positive Thinking

Just take a seat and list your failures for five reasons. Now that you are aware of what needs improvement, you may go forward with it even if it is painful.

How Often Should I Workout?

Every time you fail, try again, because doing so will make your life simpler than it has ever been. the route to failure, not failure itself!

Without this change, life would be very different.

If you don't make an effort to alter this, then be ready for a life of self-loathing and low self-esteem. Solutions are made possible by looking back at failure.

Living Through This Change

It will be much simpler to continue on the correct path if you examine and analyze your successes and failures. Additionally, it will significantly raise the likelihood of finding a durable answer.

Mind Tricks

Why will this cause me to change for the better?

How often do you just remember a short poem or other writing? This is a highly effective approach to guaranteeing that there is always a challenge for you.

Applying the Technique for More Positive Thinking

Challenges are excellent for teaching us important lessons and life lessons. Every morning, print out a poem from the internet, and try to memorize the words by the end of the day.

How Frequently Should I Exercise?

Even if you feel more at ease working with one poem per week, do it every day. Challenges are great because they allow us to assess our own abilities and talents.

Without This Change, Life

You'll doubt your capacity to pick up new knowledge and skills. You may increase your general understanding of culture and the arts by memorizing a new poem each week.

Living Through This Change

Going this route will guarantee that you can acquire the assistance you need to demonstrate your mental and memory talents, if you are unsure they exist.

The law of attraction

Why will this cause me to change for the better?

Have you ever wished for anything to last all day? If not, you must start. Dream about your goals for the rest of the day for five to ten minutes each night.

Applying the Technique for More Positive Thinking Simply slip inside your head, and you'll realize why you're doing this—what you actually desire. You'll discover new ambitions if you let your imagination rule.

How Often Should I Workout?

each day! Every day that is not spent working toward and achieving these objectives is a day lost. Always keep a desire-based objective in mind.

Without this change, life would be very different.

You won't likely ever have a sure and important course to take. Without a clear understanding of your objectives, it will inevitably be more difficult to reach them over time.

Living Through This Change

You should find it simpler to picture and then work toward the item you desire in life if you establish a distinct area of your mind where this is handled.

Behavioral Patterns

You must have complete control over your emotions if you want to succeed. However, most individuals find it difficult to reach this stage. For that reason, in this part, I've

Some of the tips I used to get there are broken down.A solid foundation must support whatever positive acts or adjustments you make in your life; this is crucial for a stable, secure way of living.

Try some of the ideas and suggestions listed below that I used to help balance and calm your mind's craziness in order to become as influential in your life as possible!

Why Will This Help Me Become More Positive? Meditation for Success

One of the main problems I discovered when I tried to modify aspects of my personal life was that my mind was constantly busy; meditation helps.

Applying the Technique for More Positive Thinking

There is no one right method to meditate, no secret technique—this is its power. Nobody else should dictate how you do the task; only you

How Often Should I Workout?

each and every day. Meditation has enabled me to purge my mind of clutter and cultivate a more positive outlook, and it has been the single biggest shift I have ever made in my life.

Without this change, life would be very different.

After you've meditated, you won't want to return to that either, as I sincerely don't want to. When you meditate, your ability to focus, be motivated, and succeed generally soars.

Living Through This Change

The change this will bring about in life is like a brand new beginning; it completely altered my perspective of the world. I'm happier and take things more seriously now.

Why Will This Help Me Become More Positive? Diaphragmatic Breathing

Since I started using diaphragmatic breathing two years ago, it has enabled me to calm down, assess my situation, and respond to it in a responsible, adult way.

Applying the Technique for More Positive Thinking

All you have to do is learn to breathe deeply and slowly.

Since everyone has a different choice for duration and depth, search online for instructions on diaphragmatic breathing that suit your preferences.

How Often Should I Workout?

Every single day—if you master this breathing method, you'll want to practice it constantly. It's a fantastic way to unwind and temporarily escape from your problems.

Without this change, life would be very different.

I noticed that my days were busier and that I kept running into issues. This enables me to approach challenges analytically.

Living Through This Change

I am happier, healthier, and more alert than ever before. I also feel more secure in difficult situations.

Walking Introspection

Why will this cause me to change for the better?

I've started practicing daily walking meditation, which is a basic method I was taught by a buddy and have been doing every day.

Applying the Technique for More Positive Thinking

Checking out this tutorial is the simplest approach to learning about walking meditation. The guide will show you how it may benefit you generally and enhance function.

How Often Should I Workout?

I essentially did this every day for two months. As a result, I began to significantly alter my approach to work and quickly develop a greater level of confidence with challenging issues.

Without this change, life would be very different.

Without this adjustment, I think I would still be pretty inconsistent and more prone to make mistakes that may have been prevented. This type of meditation makes it simpler to achieve mental clarity while being busy.

Living Through This Change

Now, when I approach difficulties with a relaxed, centered mind, they aren't quite as much of a barrier.

Recognizing Emotions

Why will this cause me to change for the better?

The challenge of expressing and comprehending our feelings is a significant problem that I and many others experience. Does this issue seem like one you are dealing with?

Simple identification is therefore helpful.

Applying the Technique for More Positive Thinking

Decide on four or five words to best express your feelings, then look up each one online. This makes it simpler for me to recognize my emotional state.

How Often Should I Workout?

This is something I now do every day to figure out where I am in my head. It may just take a slight change in perspective to make it simpler to solve an issue quickly.

Without this change, life would be very different.

It's difficult to live without this type of change; I would struggle to go back. However, the biggest benefit is that it makes it possible for me to understand how I truly feel.

Living Through This Change

I am now more capable of thinking things through before acting, which makes me less likely to respond badly to a situation.

Combining Different Perspectives

Why will this cause me to change for the better?

One of the most crucial things I can do on those days when pessimism is dominating is to take ten minutes to step back and consider the bigger picture, which will help me appreciate both success and failure.

Applying the Technique for More Positive Thinking

This is important to me since it's so simple to do; just look at your own scenario and Google it. You'll undoubtedly discover someone stuck in a far worse predicament who is unable to escape it.

How Often Should I Workout?

When I don't feel like I can conjure any optimism, I do this. Putting things in perspective allows us to see how much we seem to be exaggerating things.

Without this change, life would be very different.

Life would be really difficult right now if we didn't go through this transformation! It may be quite powerful to convey my fears in such a straightforward way.

Living Through This Change

I'm now more inclined to persevere, fight through, and come up with a proactive solution rather than getting caught up in invalidated wallowing.

5-Minute Intervals

Why Will This Make Me Positively Change?

How often do you feel like your mind is fried, yet you still attempt to work? My life has been spent doing this for countless hours. You may circumvent this issue by just pausing for a five-minute break.

Applying the Technique for More Positive Thinking

Applying the break is simple; just turn off the computer, lock it, and close your eyes. Simply shut your eyes for a short period of time while working physically.

How Frequently Should I Exercise?

It finally became a habit since I used to do it almost every day. Every hour you work, take a brief five-minute break to enable your eyes to adjust before moving on.

Without This Change, Life

When you're weary, you'll probably work at half your potential, which is a typical reason why we all feel bad.

Living Through This Change

If you make this change, you will be more precise while working and far less likely to continue making mistakes.

Because of your food

Why will this cause me to change for the better?

Many of us blame our bodies for gaining weight. Positive thinking may easily get off to a good start by acknowledging the important role that food plays in our lives.

Applying the Technique for More Positive Thinking

The concept is straightforward: consider how much what you eat affects how you feel. After all, what we eat affects how we feel throughout the day!

How Frequently Should I Exercise?

Make short notes on how you felt over the two-week period as well as the foods you consumed. Keep track of how your eating seems to be influencing or restricting your emotions and if that needs to change.

Without This Change, Life

The reality of life without this shift might be very difficult to accept. You won't address the cause of your feelings, which will worsen both your lack of movement and your general quality of life.

Living Through This Change

Simply put, eating well makes life simpler! Your body will undoubtedly function better throughout the day if you provide it with the right kind of nutrition and support. It will be easier to deal with issues and negativity if we nourish our bodies properly. If there is one aspect of life you should incorporate, it's diet planning!

Why Will This Help Me Become More Positive? Handling negative emotions

It's healthier for the mind and the spirit to deal with bad feelings and figure out why they exist than to simply let them fester. Keep in mind that these feelings are fleeting.

Applying the Technique for More Positive Thinking

Remind yourself that this kind of mental road only lasts for a short period of time if you find yourself starting down it. Sadness never lasts forever, particularly if one has an attitude that discourages it.

How Frequently Should I Exercise?

whenever you are depressed or unhappy. Later on, life gets a lot simpler the more you remind yourself that it's only a momentary mood and not how you always feel.

Without This Change, Life

You'll probably continue to believe that your day should be determined by your current feelings. This method of harnessing emotions severely restricts how far you can go.

Living Through This Change

Making the adjustment, however, makes it less probable for unpleasant emotions to hold you back since you know that they will eventually pass.

Outside, Sitting

Why will this cause me to change for the better?

Even 10 minutes spent in nature may serve as a reminder of how wonderful our world can be when we stop focusing on the bad things going on around us.

Applying the Technique for More Positive Thinking

The simplest yet—just walk outdoors and relax! Leave your phone at home and focus only on your surroundings. Enjoy the peace and quiet while listening to the wildlife.

How Frequently Should I Exercise?

whenever you have the time and the weather is suitable. Going outside may be an excellent way to simply observe the world and allow your thoughts to clear.

Without This Change, Life

You'll keep leading a strictly in-and-out lifestyle. Try to focus on less binary thinking and spend some time each day outdoors, taking in reality.

Living Through This Change

This makes a significant difference in thinking since it should be much simpler to appreciate where you are as a person and to help your thoughts slow down a little.

Mental Refocusing

Why will this cause me to change for the better?

Do you ever find yourself beginning with the negative?Then consider the ideas that preceded the negativity. What led to it?

Applying the Technique for More Positive Thinking Basically, I discovered that I might find remedies and steer clear of it in the future by just examining what led me in a bad direction.

How Often Should I Workout?

It's difficult; in my opinion, it occurs often. But it may be really helpful to just shift the focus from the misery of an issue to the reason it happened.

Without this change, life would be very different.

You won't stop feeling irritated and furious; you won't stop to consider why negativity prevails.

Living Through This Change

If you make a change, you may start tackling pessimism and identifying its root causes.

Affective Patterns

We wish to encourage individuals to think about and comprehend the significance of values in this group. Good living habits are sometimes taken for granted, but as this section will demonstrate, they may be a vital quality to take into account.

The sort of assistance you need to guarantee that your lifestyle can keep improving will be available to you if you have a strong variety of daily routines. I discovered that each of these routines helped me increase my positivity and productivity at work and at home, guaranteeing that my day-to-day would become better over time.

What do you stand for?

Why will this cause me to change for the better?

Uncertainty about our values is another prevalent problem. Having values helps in defining where we want to go and, most importantly, if our mindsets permit it.

Applying the Technique for More Positive Thinking

The greatest thing I've ever done was try to shift my perspective. Make sure that the roles you wish to play in life are reflected in your fundamental choices and ideals.

How Often Should I Workout?

It's a challenging one that requires much self-examination. However, consider your fundamental beliefs and see how they are reflected in your environment.

Without this change, life would be very different.

The majority of individuals will just live day to day without having or being aware of their core principles, never actually getting closer to being who they want to be. They may advance, but never to their desired destination.

Living Through This Change

If you begin to make decisions based on whether something meets our principles, you will become psychologically stronger and more committed to achieving your goals and dreams.

What are Your Passions?

Why will this cause me to change for the better?

I realized that by finally clarifying what my genuine interests in life were, I could be a lot more comfortable with who I was. My path, my ambitions, and my desires became clearer.

Applying the Technique for More Positive Thinking

To implement this activity, I just looked at what gave my stomach a shock when I thought about it. This sensation leads me to want to find out more about myself.

How Often Should I Workout?

Every minute of every day—your passions should never be forgotten.

Every morning, simply take half an hour to think about how today will help you advance towards eventually realizing your desire.

Without this change, life would be very different.

You'll just go from one day, one week, and one year to the next. You'll never define or better yourself, and you'll probably always have a pessimistic mindset.

Living Through This Change

However, by employing this, you increase your chances of success since you are clear on your objectives for now and the future.

Establishing a Vision

Why will this cause me to change for the better?

The most influential individuals have a vision or a dream. Make sure you have a clear picture of where you want to go, including a successful role model.

Applying the Technique for More Positive Thinking

It's crucial to follow through with this since doing so guarantees your ongoing success. Applying that step just entails spending the morning planning out your life's goals.

How Often Should I Workout?

daily, if you can! Knowing your life's goal and purpose is one of the most powerful things you can do. You may concentrate for the next week during that half an hour.

Without this change, life would be very different.

Without taking the effort to identify what our passions and energy will be motivated by, we just muddle through each day.

Living Through This Change

However, if you make this change, you will experience consistent reaction and advancement because you will be more motivated and actively interested in achieving your goals.

Self-motivation: Why will this make me happier?

I discovered that thinking about all the achievements you have already achieved is the simplest method to motivate yourself. How can you achieve that level of accomplishment once again?

Applying the Technique for More Positive Thinking

To do this, all you need to do is reflect on your past. Describe your journey there. How were you feeling? What prevents you from experiencing the same success today?

How Often Should I Workout?

Never stop looking for the answer that will shape your future, planning for it, or preparing for it. You can go again only by remembering what previously motivated you.

Without this change, life would be very different.

Before I had truly tried to motivate myself with past successes, my life was really challenging. My self-esteem was destroyed, and I was convinced that chance was the only factor in any achievement.

Living Through This Change

But ever since I've had the opportunity, I tend to replicate my previous triumphs rather often.

When I do things now, I often discover that my previous success was motivated by a desire that is no longer there.

Questioning Beliefs

Why will this cause me to change for the better?

How often do you act contrary to a notion you hold? Recently, I began to argue with myself and refute my own arguments, and it's been huge.

Applying the Technique for More Positive Thinking

Just go through a typical debate you would have. What argument do you support? What is the primary objection? Utilizing this enables you to evaluate your level of consideration.

How Often Should I Workout?

Every time! It will be crucial to simply understand how to put such ideals into practice. You also fill in the gaps in your reasoning by being aware of how others could respond.

Without this change, life would be very different.

You'll simply keep holding the same positions until you're pressed and embarrassed.

Are you willing to put up the effort required to pursue knowledge and success?

Living Through This Change

But the glass ceiling is broken when you allow this transformation to occur. Finding honest and realistic replies to your questions and concerns will be simpler for you.

Giving up

Why will this cause me to change for the better?

Many of us, including myself, are constrained by our material possessions.

Loss phobia makes us ruthless, from our TVs to our vehicles. The first step toward normalcy is losing it.

Applying the Technique for More Positive Thinking

It was difficult, but I had to just start giving things away to learn that life continued after that item left the home.

How Often Should I Workout?

Every week thus far, I've given something valuable to me to a friend, a member of my family, or a charity. It's making me realize that there's more to life than sitting on a couch!

Without this change, life would be very different.

Without making this adjustment, I discovered that I just stayed suspicious and pessimistic. Instead of fostering ambition, my fear of losing the things I loved most led me to conservatism.

Living Through This Change

When I decided to donate my belongings, I felt a sense of emotional liberation. You may easily be ambitious in other ways if you give it a try for yourself.

self-centered or selfless?

Why Will This Make Me Positively Change?

Continuing from the previous point, deciding whether you should be selfish or selfless is a popular choice for ensuring that you make wise decisions in the near future.

Applying the Technique for More Positive Thinking

Try to compare how you feel when you choose a course of action that benefits others while hindering you to see which one makes you feel better. What improved your mood? You aspire to be the sort of person described here.

How Frequently Should I Exercise?

Try again and again until you succeed. There are several methods to test which kind of mental plan works best for you, from purchasing something you don't need to giving up a week's pay.

Without This Change, Life

You'll most likely feel much more at ease with who you are after taking the time to accomplish this. It'll probably also ensure that you are aware of the kinds of goals you need to have. A selfish goal cannot be attained by practicing selflessness along the way!

Living Through This Change

On the other hand, if you wish to be unselfish and constantly behave selfishly, you cannot assist yourself enough. It takes effort to find the approach that you think works best for you, but once you do, you'll feel more optimistic and confident about who you are.

Cutting yourself off

Why will this cause me to change for the better?

How often do you feel like you undersell yourself? I used to constantly discover that my skills were constrained by my pessimistic perspective on life.

Applying the Technique for More Positive Thinking

I just needed to take a closer look at the decision-making process to alter that. I immediately became aware of how often I made decisions based only on the whims of others.

How Frequently Should I Exercise?

I began making judgments the other way as a matter of practice. In the past, I would prioritize my needs above those of others and vice versa.

Without This Change, Life Prior to this, I realized that I often sacrificed my own happiness in an attempt to make others happy.

Living Through This Change

However, I find that these days I'm a lot more at ease making decisions based on what I want to accomplish rather than always attempting to appease other people.

Avoiding Excuses

Why Will This Make Me Positively Change?

I had a serious mental health issue where I was always seeking justifications to keep from having to face failure. I focused on my mistakes in an effort to fix this.

Applying the Technique for More Positive Thinking

I began to consider the reasons why things went wrong and what role I specifically played in them. It was the best course of action I could have chosen because now that I can clearly see where I went wrong, I can stop blaming others.

How Frequently Should I Exercise?

The additional practice has made sure I keep improving, and it has really helped me come to grips with who I am. I'd advise doing this if you catch yourself rationalizing a subpar performance or careless error on your part.

Without This Change, Life

I had a very uncertain existence until I truly began to consider my own actions before those of others. I would feel vulnerable around everyone and safe around no one.

Living Through This Change

Now that I can identify my flaws, I feel much more at ease and optimistic than I previously did.

making, rather than responding

Why Will This Make Me Positively Change?

I've discovered that creating is the most effective method to deal with negativity. I have now put that power to good use.

Applying the Technique for More Positive Thinking Applying is simple; just start a hobby. Instead of reacting when things go wrong, turn to your interests.

How Often Should I Workout?

This makes it quite simple to give yourself some thought before responding, allowing your emotions to be guided by creativity.

Without this change, life would be very different.

I used to respond badly to a lot of circumstances, which would lead to conflict with other people.

Living Through This Change

Now I spend time thinking about what went wrong, bringing about greater unity.

Personal Practices

Okay, so in this part, we're going to look into adaptable personal behaviors. The majority of these are designed with business productivity in mind. A prosperous, energetic, and busy business life, in my opinion, is the most helpful mark you can make on your life!

Why Will This Help Me Become More Positive? Simplifying Your Day

The simplest method to make your days simpler is to arrange everything and then clean up the clutter so you can work without interruption.

Applying the Technique for More Positive Thinking

Starting an hour before you need to be productive in the morning is the simplest way to do this. You can focus only on having fun and maximizing your day when there is no clutter to distract you.

How Often Should I Workout?

You'll experience great advantages if you do this each morning. This works in both the business world and the home.

Without this change, life would be very different.

You'll probably find that you have a lot of trouble keeping organized if you don't take this step. The state of the location then dictates the days.

Living Through This Change

It is obvious that this move would make your life simpler; the only catch is that you will need to put in an hour of preparation time. The added benefit is a much simpler way of living that makes it easier to focus.

Identifying Your Goals

Why will this cause me to change for the better?

For both of us, setting objectives will now be the finest part of every endeavor. It will be a lot simpler for you to go ahead if you prioritize your primary objectives by starting with the most difficult.

Applying the Technique for More Positive Thinking

This may be implemented most easily in the morning or the night before.

Simply make a strategy for the job you think will be the most challenging and focus on it first.

How Often Should I Workout?

You may focus on the easy tasks for the remainder of the day if you finish the toughest job each day. Putting off more difficult tasks until later is a recipe for disaster!

Without this change, life would be very different.

I was never efficient enough, and as a consequence, my intelligence would suffer.

My company was unable to govern itself and maintain the proper formula, and I discovered that every day would turn into an unpredictable fight that was difficult to handle.

Living Through This Change

Instead, you may adopt this method of thinking, which is so much more effective that it almost defies belief. I spent my morning dealing with the bigger issues, so now I have the rest of the day to address the little ones!

Starting a Project: Why Will Being More Positive as a Result Help Me?

Making a project with a plan was one of the most original methods I've discovered to get inspiration for my goals and aspirations. It helps to work nonstop for 30 minutes each day!

Applying the Technique for More Positive Thinking, I would work furiously on the assignment within this thirty-minute window, then return the following day. It made it possible for me to focus on side projects without being impatient or concerned that I was wasting time.

How Often Should I Workout?

I do this action once per day, or twice if it's a slow day. Working on a side project while doing other things makes it much simpler to grasp and appreciate where I am at with it.

Without this change, life would be very different.

Without it, I would just keep making the same mistakes. I would often start two projects at once and finish barely 50% of each. I now give each project my all at the designated times.

Living Through This Change

Since I oversaw this project, every single aspect of my life has improved. My business' consistency has increased as a result!

Creating Habits

Why Will This Make Me Positively Change?

Developing more optimistic behaviors played a significant role in my change from optimism to negativity. For instance, I eliminated work-related distractions like cellphones, clutter, and laptops.

Applying the Technique for More Positive Thinking

I discovered that by doing this, my days were much more productive. I would work much harder if I eliminate distractions—even by simply turning my phone to silent and laying it face down.

How Frequently Should I Exercise?

If you apply this to your daily job, all of life's unpleasant issues will disappear. With this mindset, productivity and optimistic thinking rise, ensuring you'll keep evolving and adapting to deal with issues head-on.

Without This Change, Life

I discovered that my life before this was utterly disorganized. I would always spend an hour on Twitter to get through the day; fortunately, those issues are resolved today.

Living Through This Change

Now, I can do hours' worth of work without stopping.

I don't let my thoughts wander, which keeps me focused and helps me feel less pessimistic than previously.

How to Measure Productivity

Why Will This Make Me Positively Change?

The greatest advice I can give everyone reading this to increase productivity is to consider how you are currently at work—do you whine?

Applying the Technique for More Positive Thinking

If you tend to constantly find something to complain about, try to figure out why. Why are you feeling that way? What is the other viewpoint, too?

How Frequently Should I Exercise?

When I consider how other people might interpret the image, this was a huge help to me. My whining would quickly end if I was just honest with myself when I complained.

Without This Change, Life

Really, it's that easy, yet without this modification, I would never have been able to work harder. I would constantly give up at the first obstacle and never try to get over it.

Living Through This Change

With time, this adjustment became much more straightforward and efficient. I quickly came to see that whining was a waste of time and energy that might have been used for something constructive.

Using Batch for Success

Why will this cause me to change for the better?

The greatest way I've discovered to make my days simpler and happier is to batch chores. As a result, I was able to produce more with each hour I put in.

Applying the Technique for More Positive Thinking

How so? because I had shifted in my thinking. I soon realized that tasks were being completed by ensuring that items 1-4 were completed prior to a longer break rather than just 1.

How Often Should I Workout?

I decided to live in this manner moving forward. It quickly became a significant component of my daily and overall planning, ensuring that I always completed related chores at the same time.

Without this change, life would be very different.

Without making any changes, I would continue to live a life driven by negativity. In my opinion, the smallest disruption to my imagined schedule would destroy my day and make chores take longer.

Living Through This Change

I also discovered that switching to this approach made it simpler for me to complete things. Now, all comparable activities would be grouped together and completed quickly.

Making Priorities

Why will this cause me to change for the better?

Making a range and list of priorities made it much easier for me to get where I needed to go in life and kept my days from becoming overly hectic.

Applying the Technique for More Positive Thinking

I would write out a list of the events that would take place the next day, along with estimated time frames for each, an hour before going to bed. This made planning easier.

How Often Should I Workout?

I am now making practicing this at night a significant portion of my day. In order to observe how I responded to deadlines like these, I would make sure that my plans became ever more strict.

Without this change, life would be very different.

I would just be disorganized, having "good days" and "bad days," causing my workload to mount to the point that it was practically impossible to manage afterwards.

Living Through This Change

But now, what? I can live a happy life since I am aware of the consistency of my days. Even if there are fewer "good days," the "terrible days" are over!

Why will rising earlier help me become more positive?

One of the most beneficial things I have ever done was just set my alarm for an hour earlier, since that additional hour makes such a difference in the morning.

Applying the Technique for More Positive Thinking

My alarm was recently changed by one hour. Being up an hour earlier makes me more productive and gives me the essential time I need to wake up before work.

How Often Should I Workout?

I now do this action daily. It has been a cornerstone in bringing about every other constructive activity in this book, guaranteeing that I may keep modifying and bettering my mindset to suit what is required.

Without this change, life would be very different.

Without altering the time I woke up, life would continue to be stressful. I used to arrive at work while still half asleep and discover that production had decreased during the day.

Living Through This Change

However, this adjustment made it simple for me to steer clear of this issue and begin working more consistently and optimistically.

Utilizing bulk work

Why will this cause me to change for the better?

I discovered that working in larger chunks of 3–4 hours at a time with fewer breaks was easier than working in small groups and doing portions.

Applying the Technique for More Positive Thinking

The justification was really straightforward: if I applied this to my day, I would be more successful, happier, and more likely to maintain a constant level of performance rather than peaking and plummeting.

How Often Should I Workout?

For the remainder of my life, I will just incorporate this into my daily plans.

I now work in larger sections and take longer, more leisurely breaks.

Without this change, life would be very different.

In the past, I would squeeze in work to get to a quick break and then spend the whole break freaking out. I can now unwind and wait for the remainder of the day to begin.

Living Through This Change

I've been more forceful and productive at work as a result of this adjustment. Now, regardless of the challenge, I'm far less inclined to approach my day negatively.

Why will learning to say no make me more positive?

Saying no to people has always been a big problem for me. It may be difficult, and I used to simply go along with situations that made me quite miserable.

Applying the Technique for More Positive Thinking

To combat this, I simply began to refuse. It seems easy, but the more I forced it the first time, the simpler it became each subsequent time.

How Often Should I Workout?

I was always approving of things that I couldn't or shouldn't be doing. It increased my comfort level and my relationships with many different individuals on a social and professional level.

Without this change, life would be very different.

Without this transformation, life was really difficult for me since I often made errors or found myself in challenging circumstances that I did not have the skills or expertise to manage.

Living Through This Change

I feel more in charge of my future and more confident than ever right now.

I've stopped making the same error and am now living the life I had planned!

www.ingramcontent.com/pod-product-compliance
Lightning Source LLC
Chambersburg PA
CBHW071146220526
45467CB00015B/2014